May 12 2004

To My Dear Joan
With Best Wishes on your Brid
Love Joan.
x x

Keighley & Worth Valley Railway

Michael Harris

Ian Allan PUBLISHING

First published 1998

ISBN 0 7110 2631 9

© Ian Allan Publishing Ltd 1998

Published by Ian Allan Publishing

an imprint of Ian Allan Publishing Ltd, Terminal House,
Station Approach, Shepperton, Surrey TW17 8AS.
Printed by Ian Allan Printing Ltd, Riverdene Business
Park, Molesey Road, Hersham, Surrey KT12 4RG.

Code: 9809/A

Previous page:
Bellerophon *climbs Ingrow bank on 15 March 1987.*
D. Stuart Lindsay

Below:
Haworth locomotive depot on 25 February 1988.
D. Stuart Lindsey

Front cover:
*No 78022 departs Oakworth with a Oxenhope train on 22 March
1998.* Kevin Truby

Back cover:
*Out from Ingrow Tunnel comes ex-Midland Railway '4F' 0-6-0
No 43924. A March 1979 picture.* John Cooper-Smith

Back cover, inset:
*LNWR No 1054 leads a rake of historic coaches out of
Oxenhope, 10 May 1998.*
Chris Dixon

Contents

Thirty years ago the Keighley & Worth Valley was front page news. The reason was simple: industrial action meant that British Railways was not running any trains on the very day that this new preserved railway was launching its public service. In another way it was prophetic because the newcomer was promoting itself as a steam railway when BR was entering its final month of steam operation on the standard gauge.

It was this cross-over between steam as a regular phenomenon on our national railways and the emergence of the steam railway as a public attraction which placed the K&WVR in the centre of many railway people's affections. Over the last 30 years the Railway has often been at the forefront of developments but it has always remained true to its original principles, its roots and its people. Those in charge have never forgotten that the preserved Railway got off the ground because local people were determined that the line for which their forebears had fought to get built should not end up as a disused trail along the bottom of the Worth Valley. That is one of the themes in this book.

Introduction

It does not pretend to be an exhaustive, blow by blow history of the Keighley & Worth Valley, neither of the original company which died in the last century, nor of the current operating company, the Keighley & Worth Valley Light Railway Ltd, nor of the Preservation Society.

Rather it is an attempt at a time of anniversary to highlight some of the achievements, realities perhaps, that seemed relevant to me as author. It is written not from the point of someone directly involved but from that of a respectful bystander. That was how I felt when I travelled over from York in 1966 to see just what they were doing in Haworth yard. You could appreciate that they had a long way to go but at least they had got stuck in.

Over the past 20 years I have been able to spend more time at the Railway having a closer look, and hearing first-hand what is being planned. I've appreciated that and in return I hope that this book will do the Railway some good.

It's impossible to predict where railway preservation might go in the future. As those of us who can recall everyday steam working grow older, will railway preservation suffer or even decline because the feeling which so many of us had back in 1968 that steam should not perish is no longer a primary motivation?

The best one can say is that it seems unlikely because the preserved railways have become part of the wider community rather than just commemorating the enthusiasm of a minority.

I was reminded of that when my wife and I were travelling on one of the K&WVR's Spring Enthusiasts' Weekend trains and observing a youngster, no more than three or four years of age, who was completely engrossed by a small model of one of Thomas the Tank Engine's shed-mates. That someone born 30 years after steam ceased to be an everyday experience for people in this country should be so interested, not only in the model but in the full-size Worth Valley engines and the trains, seemed not only rather touching but led us to think that whatever happens in the future there will be plenty like him to which steam means *something*. But would Thomas have become so popular in recent years if there had not been a Keighley & Worth Valley, or others like it?

Michael Harris,
Ottershaw, Surrey
May 1998

Even today, when we take the ability to move about wherever we want for granted, the Pennines remain an effective barrier to movement. Glance at an Ordnance Survey map and west of the built-up area of Bradford and West Yorkshire there seems to be a hilly wilderness. Look closer, near where an upside-down 'N' of Pennine appears on the map, and the name Oxenhope appears. This is the head of a valley stretching just over four miles to Keighley, an industrial town in the Aire Valley, along which the River Aire flows eastwards at right-angles to the axis of the Pennines.

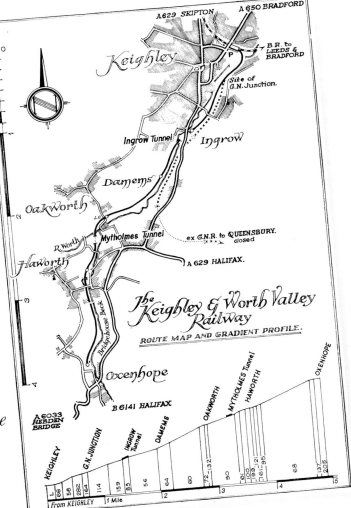

1: *A Railway for the* Worth Valley

We have become so used to speaking of the 'Keighley & Worth Valley' that most people do not realise that only the first part of the valley is truly the Worth Valley. The River Worth has a tributary and it is alongside this, the Bridgehouse Beck, that the Worth Valley's railway travels to its terminus at Oxenhope.

Why stop there you might ask? Overlooked by Keighley Moor, the River Worth itself heads off in the direction of Colne, but the Bridgehouse Beck goes along a narrower valley, along which there were mills.

The earliest thoughts of a railway along the Worth Valley date back to 1845, when the idea had been to link Hebden Bridge, on the River Calder and to the south of Oxenhope, with both Haworth and Keighley. They would have achieved it by tunnelling under Oxenhope Moor. But the promoters of the scheme chose a bad time to raise money and so their plans came to nothing.

Nowadays, it is difficult to imagine that the communities along the Worth Valley contributed to Britain's Industrial Revolution. The area hardly seems tainted by factories today and, when walking along the valley side from Oxenhope to Haworth, you are as much in the countryside as almost anywhere else in Britain.

Well into the 16th century the spinning and weaving of wool had begun in moorland farmhouses, and gradually the weavers collected into settlements. By the 18th century weaving communities such as that at Haworth may well have been on the edge of wild moorlands and at first sight remote from their neighbours but they were linked by pack-horse trails which were used to take finished cloth to markets in the larger towns. A

Below:
Keighley station, c1905.
Real Photographs (28248)

century later and it was clear that the weaving mills could reduce their costs by using rail to transport their product while the coal and other materials needed by the new steam-mills could be brought in more easily.

That seemed obvious to the mill-owners but the Midland Railway, a constituent company of which had brought the railway to Keighley from Leeds in 1847, was happy to handle the incoming coal and other necessities at Keighley, from where horse-drawn transport would distribute them and collect the finished cloth for market. There had been a plan for a branch railway to Haworth but it had not materialised. Instead, the mill-owners, local businessmen and 'movers and shakers' of the Worth Valley decided they would promote a railway themselves. They tried but failed in 1853: the Midland Railway remained uninterested. Not for the first time in this story local initiative was needed to put the Worth Valley on the map.

The history of our railways is to be found as much in musty, leather-bound minute-books and ledgers filled with copper-plate handwriting as in the more obvious memorials of sturdy stone-built stations and the relatively few surviving steam locomotives, coaches and wagons from Victorian days.

Nowadays the irreplaceable records of the old companies are held in the Public Record office at Kew, or county record offices. Enquire at Kew for archive RAIL 331/1 and you will be handed the minute book of the original Keighley & Worth Valley Railway (K&WVR Co).

Start at the beginning and you will see a circular from Messrs Weatherhead & Burr headed 'Keighley 28th August 1861' and 'Proposed Haworth Railway'. Recipients of the circular were invited to a meeting at the *Black Bull Inn*, Haworth on Friday, 13 September at 3 o'clock 'convened for the purpose of considering and determining if any (and what) steps shall now be taken to obtain to Haworth and the Vale of the Worth the advantages of that Railway communication it so much requires.'

That historic meeting did not take place until 8 October 1861. It proved to be the starting-point of the Worth Valley Railway. Jonathan N. Craven both moved and seconded a resolution which was carried unanimously, 'That this meeting being fully convinced that a Railway from Keighley to Haworth is necessary for the maintenance of the present value of property, the general welfare of the Locality and the industrial progress, pledges itself to subscribe and to obtain subscribers for the accomplishment of the object, being convinced that it will form a good investment of capital, and that the question of its prolongation to Lowertown depends upon its Survey, and probable traffic and subscription.' Lowertown is the community surrounding today's station at Oxenhope. As with so many other railways, the line actually stops short of the place it is advertised as serving!

The very formal language of documents such as this may make us smile today. We may not share notions of 'industrial progress' and are unlikely to talk in terms of a 'good investment of capital'. Yet such motivations in Victorian society caused the railway system to be constructed. Because, to put it crudely, the people attending the meeting at Haworth on 8 October 1861 put their money where their mouths were.

Resolution No 2 at the meeting recorded that seven of those present pledged themselves to take shares in the enterprise. Jonas Sugden and Brothers and Jonathan N. Craven respectively committed themselves to £5,000; the Merrall Brothers and Sir Isaac Holden (the MP for Keighley) each signed up for £2,500. Three other persons at the meeting pledged themselves to a total of £420: small by comparison maybe but still quite a lot in today's money. All these people were investing in £5 shares with the object of taking the railway to Haworth. George Gregson, however, had put his name down for 50 shares 'in favour of its (the Railway) going to Lowertown'.

**Worth Valley
Stations in Midland
Days, c1905.**
Above:
Ingrow.
Real Photographs (28245)

Right:
*Damems, but later than
1905. Upon closure the
original buildings were
removed.*
J. Stobbs

At the *Black Bull Inn* meeting of October 1861 it was agreed to form a committee to canvass for further subscribers in order to raise capital for the railway project. A month later it was decided that the 'Proposed Railway' should have a terminus at Oxenhope Mill and that there should be a road from there to Lowertown. By now, 1,255 shares had been subscribed to, with a total value of £6,275. These were local people investing hard-earned savings in a public enterprise.

An Otley civil engineer, John MacLandsborough reported at a meeting at the *Black Bull Inn*, Haworth a week later, on 16 October 1861, that he had surveyed the line from Bridgehouse to Lowertown and had arrived at an estimate for the railway to Oxenhope Mill and the connecting road. The next stage was to approach the local landowners and to begin the process of negotiation to arrive at the terms by which they would sell their land to the railway.

Two months later, just five days before Christmas 1861, the *Black Bull*, Haworth was again the location of a railway meeting, and by now there was a provisional board of directors. They were petitioning the Government for leave to bring in a Bill for construction of the railway, and on the table there was a draft heads of agreement with the Midland Railway. That was to ensure the connection with the main line at Keighley among other things. The railway along the Worth Valley was on the point of becoming a reality.

The directors gave both of their money and of their time for, apart from receiving £50 expenses, they agreed they would not be paid other allowances or compensated for time spent away from their day to day employment. This, and the election of directors, and the appointment of a company secretary, auditors and bankers was agreed at the first general or ordinary meeting of what was now called The Keighley and Worth Valley Railway Company. Again, the *Black Bull Inn*, Haworth was the chosen location and the meeting was held on the day before Christmas Eve, 1862. Perhaps we can imagine the sense of pride when, to quote, it was 'Resolved that the seal now produced and exhibited for Inspection be adopted as the seal of the said Company'.

A week later, the newly elected directors met for the first time and all resolved that Isaac Holden (he was later knighted) should be Company Chairman in succession to George Oats Greenwood who had been acting Chairman for the first year of the enterprise.

Now came the first stages in building the railway. Land had to be acquired and a contractor chosen to construct the line. Tenders had to be drawn up and issued so that a supplier of track materials could be chosen. The junction with the Midland Railway had to be arranged. All this was done.

The ceremonial cutting of the first sod took place on 9 February 1864. As the K&WVR Co was a local enterprise, very much controlled by people in the locality, the directors had to exercise their judgement as to whether the railway was being constructed as they wanted. Yet, as far as one can tell, none of them was an expert on railways.

Late December 1864 and the directors asked for the engineer to direct his attention to the 'Cutting through the road called Ebor Lane for the intended bridge is in a very dangerous state'. At a subsequent meeting it was suggested that 'some competent person' should 'visit and inspect the works on the line occasionally as necessity required and to make suggestions and complaints to the Contractor (if found necessary). Mr Jonathan N. Craven was accordingly named...'. The railway contractor was a John Metcalfe.

All these aspects — the involvement of local and public-spirited individuals without professional knowledge of railways and their operation — were to find a parallel a century later when inhabitants were faced with trying to ensure the survival of the Worth Valley's railway.

Local and public-spirited individuals… of course, but not immune to human frailties and pomposities! Although local newspapers frequently made gentle fun of their town's railway in its early days, in the case of the K&WVR Co a local character, Bill o' th' Hoylus End (he was christened William Wight), was on hand to satirise its proceedings. His book *Th' History o' Haworth Railway* (recently republished by the Keighley & Worth Valley Preservation Society) had sold 100,000 copies by the 1890s. It tells its story in local dialect and is a welcome reminder that we need to take some of the sober historical accounts with a pinch of salt.

Reasonably enough, and like many another locally promoted railway company, the directors of the original K&WVR Co concluded an agreement with a main line company, in this case the Midland Railway, by which their line was worked the line for a proportion of the receipts, in this case 50%.

As with other new railways being built in those far-off days of the 1860s, and indeed previous to that, one of the most difficult issues was the acquisition of land together with all the various issues relating to freehold and leasehold of property and the associated legal demands. Then there was the valuation and purchase of properties and, where necessary, arrangements for their demolition. The K&WVR Co became engaged in negotiations with the Duke of Devonshire for land in the area.

Mid-1865 found the directors contemplating the allegedly dangerous state of the Wesley Place Chapel which might have to be closed 'for sacred worship' upon the opening of the line. In an area with strong support for non-Conformism this had the potential to be a serious matter. The railway directors concluded that the chapel was 'placed with insufficient foundations upon bad ground' and that it had begun to give way before construction of the railway cutting had started. The eventual upshot was that the matter was passed to an arbitrator and in due course the Company had to pay up.

The burdens of and responsibility associated with being a railway director were clearly not for the faint-hearted. Construction of what after all was a short 4¾-mile branch line did not proceed at all happily. More money was needed. July 1865, and the directors resolved at their meting that a call of £2 be made on all shares. This was by no means the final appeal for additional funding. At the same time, reference was made to the progress with the line's construction, 'great dissatisfaction being felt and expressed that the same was not pushed on with that vigour and speed desired especially that part of the works connected with Paper Mill Bridge and Ebor Bridge…'. The directors (and indeed the shareholders) must have wondered where their money was going — and to what end. Materials for the track had been delivered but there was concern that they were either being lost, damaged, or used for 'different' purposes.

At their October 1866 meeting the directors were of one mind, being 'thoroughly convinced that the line might be opened by the first day of November next if the contractor will only push on the works in a proper spirit. The Engineer was given 'special instructions' 'to cause all the Works to be completed by the above named time…'. Sadly, a violent storm in mid-November 1866 swept away some of the embankment between Oakworth and Damems and delayed the opening of the line by six months.

Eventually, the Keighley & Worth Valley Railway had its ceremonial and official opening on Saturday, 13 April 1867. The inaugural train experienced an embarrassingly awful run over the uphill grades from Keighley, during which it had to be divided in order for the engine to take the train beyond Oakworth.

Two days after the opening the Midland Railway assumed responsibility for operating the regular passenger service, and goods traffic, really the mainspring of the railway, began passing over the line from 1 July 1867. For its first year the line was maintained by the contractor.

At last some revenue was coming in. Finished cloth was now moving from mills in the valley, and coal was being brought in return, to fuel the boilers of the factory steam engines. Not only that: because coal could now be conveyed cheaply to the Worth valley, gasworks were built both at Haworth and Oakworth, to supply local households. That was what the construction of local railways was all about. They had a real effect on everyone's lives.

Starting from Keighley, the original stations on the branch were at Ingrow, Oakworth, Haworth and Oxenhope. At their meeting on 25 June 1867 the K&WVR Co directors agreed to make a platform at Damems '30 yards long and 2 yards broad'. By October 1867 all the line's stations were available for traffic, and operations settled down to a steady routine. In these early years there were usually six passenger trains each way on weekdays, and four on Sundays. The directors contented themselves with the mundane housekeeping of a railway. At the meeting on 20 August 1867 they instructed that 'all thistles must be mown and cleared away from the slopes and land belonging to the Company without further delay.'

The line to Oxenhope clearly was serving its purpose and generating revenue, and a small return for the investors, more than could be said for some railways of this period. At the ordinary and half-yearly meeting of shareholders held at the *Black Bull*, Haworth on

26 March 1870 it was decided 'that a dividend of three per cent be paid upon the Preference Shares for the year ended December 31 1869'. Meeting on 30 September 1871, as usual at the *Black Bull*, it was resolved that 'a dividend of 3 per cent per annum be paid upon the Preference Shares for the ½ year ended June 30 1871'.

As yet the dissatisfaction between the Company and the contractor regarding the problems and delay with building the railway had not been resolved. The directors pursued their claim against the contractor. At the Directors' Meeting on 27 November 1872, no less than five years after the opening of the line, Mr Metcalfe, the contractor, was present, to say that he wanted to come to some agreement and asked for the Action in Chancery to be withdrawn. No doubt thankfully, both parties decided to settle their claim, the basis of such an agreement being that each side paid their costs.

In 1864, there had been ideas of another railway being built to Keighley, also entering from the Worth Valley but the Bill to construct it was rejected by Parliament. Another attempt came in 1872, and it featured a line from Queensbury to Keighley. Because the Midland had withdrawn its support, the promoters of the Halifax, Thornton & Keighley Railway had turned instead to the competing Great Northern Railway for backing. How would the K&WVR Co react?

At their meeting on 11 February 1873 the K&WVR Co directors duly considered the potential of the new line from Queensbury. Having done so, they promised that the Company 'will assist the Midland Co in its opposition to the Halifax, Thornton and Keighley Railway Bill but will not incur any expenses in so doing. All expenses must be paid by the Midland'. Such qualified determination!

At any rate, after spending a vast sum of money to complete the lines serving Queensbury it was 1884 before the line from Thornton reached Keighley, one associated development being the opening of a new joint Great Northern and Midland station at Keighley in May 1883.

By then, K&WVR Co directors had virtually ended the independence of their railway. Back in September 1880, they had agreed that the Company seal should be affixed to an agreement with the Midland Railway Company which would bring the sale and transfer of the Railway to the larger concern. The local railway had been in dispute with the Midland and possibly its sale was as an effective way as any of concluding the matter. In the following year — 1881 — the Midland took over the Worth Valley line.

Four years were to pass before the K&WVR Co itself ceased to exist. The directors met in July 1885, to be informed that £14,500 had been received from the Midland Railway Co under the provisions of the Midland Railway (Additional Powers) Act 1881 by which the Keighley & Worth Valley Railway had been absorbed. The settlement closed all outstanding claims between the two companies. Another Directors' Meeting the following month is notable only for recording that £214 was to be paid to Jonathan Whitley, our Secretary 'for his long and faithful services to the Company and for the loss of his old office under the Company'.

One more formality had still to take place. At 3.30pm on 2 February 1886, a special meeting of the shareholders of the Worth Valley Railway Co was held in its offices at No 1 Scott Street, Keighley to record that the Midland guaranteed the payment of interest or dividends on Worth Valley stock consolidated in the Midland. The little local company was accordingly dissolved later in 1886.

Branch lines such as that along the Worth Valley generally settled down to a humdrum existence once their initial opening celebrations had been largely forgotten. But for some time after the Great Northern had reached Keighley from Queensbury and made its entrance to the town alongside the Worth Valley line, there were schemes for fantastical railways that might have changed the local maps. In 1890, for instance, came a proposal for the North West Central Railway that envisaged 13 railways linking Preston, Whalley, Colne and Keighley, branching off from the Queensbury-Keighley line south of the last-named town on its way to Colne. Such schemes were promoted too late in the railway age.

2: Lifeline for the Valley

In 1891, the Midland Railway obtained powers to replace the Vale Mill Viaduct south of Oakworth because its condition was deteriorating. A new alignment was chosen for the railway over this section. It included the 75yd Mytholmes Tunnel as well as a three-arch bridge which took the line across the River Worth and which has become a favourite location for railway photographers in recent years. The new stretch of line opened in November 1892.

Although the earliest intentions were for the line to be built with 'a double line of rails', as completed the Worth Valley was a single-track line, its capacity being further limited as it was not possible to cross trains *en route*. Loops at Oakworth and Haworth came into use in April 1900. The line had originally been operated as a single section with a train staff as authority for a train to run over the branch. More modern forms of train working were introduced later, such as the electric train tablet system which came into use after 1900

although staff working was retained between Oxenhope and Haworth.

The branch line climbed steeply and continuously up the valley and the hazard of a runaway train was always present. Early on 27 September 1875, a train of goods wagons and empty passenger coaches set out for Oxenhope at dawn. At Oakworth, with the engine and its crew engaged in shunting, the other railwaymen present had failed to pin down the brakes on the stationary wagons. Before long, the wagons (less engine) were away off downhill, pursued by the engine. At Keighley station they collided with a Bradford-Colne train, some of whose passengers were injured as a result. Possibly as a consequence of the runaway the electric telegraph was installed on the branch in 1877. If it had been there two years earlier at least Keighley could have been warned of the approaching runaway train.

Below:
The Worth Valley branch is steeply graded and by the time it has reached Oxenhope the line is 660ft above sea level. This August 1983 picture of a genuine Midland Railway 0-6-0, BR No 43924, entering Oxenhope shows clearly the board (about level with the engineman) which instructs a guard on an unfitted goods that before setting off down the 1 in 66 towards Haworth 'Goods trains to stop and pin down brakes'.
Tim Grimshaw

Midland Motive Power.

Top right:

For much of its working life the line was worked by the Class 1 0-6-0Ts. Those allocated to work on the Worth Valley generally had enclosed cabs but otherwise were very similar to No 1346 shown here.
Real Photographs (28192)

Centre right:

The Johnson 0-4-4Ts became familiar power later on, and then from the mid-1930s push-pull equipped engines were used. This is non push-pull fitted LMS No 1383 which shows the appearance of these engines when fitted with a Belpaire firebox and with a modified cab.
Real Photographs (R7210)

Below right:

In later days the Class 3 0-6-0s were employed on the branch goods workings. This is a Midland era picture taken at Skipton with No 2117.
Real Photographs (28217)

The lesson of the runaway was taken to heart. In later years the LMS special instructions for the Worth Valley Branch warned 'No vehicle of a train going towards Oxenhope, which has to attach or detach traffic at Oakworth or Haworth, must be allowed to stand upon the main line at Oakworth or Haworth without the engine being attached.'

During the late 19th century, the number of regular passenger trains over the branch was increased, particularly once the passing loops were available after 1900. The line was simply worked, with tank engines and four-wheeled, later six-wheeled, compartment coaches on the passenger trains.

Because of its gradients which included the awkward curved start up the bank from Keighley station and the sections of 1 in 56-64 north of Ingrow and almost into Oakworth it was not a line to be taken for granted. Between Oxenhope and Keighley Station Junction the speed limit was 30mph, except over the Deviation line between Oakworth and Haworth where it was further restricted to 15mph.

From the earliest days the Midland Railway had used 0-6-0Ts on the branch. Five of its standard shunting engines modified with all-over cabs and vacuum brake gear were built specially for the line in 1883. Another five engines dating from 1891 were also later earmarked for use on the branch.

What were the stations like? Fortunately, most of their character has survived, although at Ingrow the present station building is in replacement of the original structure. It was removed from Foulridge for re-erection at Ingrow and is actually better in keeping with the other stations than its lost predecessor.

Contrasting views of Keighley station.
Above:
MR Johnson 4-4-0 No 82 on a main line passenger working. The train is standing at the Leeds end of the up platform.
Real Photographs (28159)

Left:
Keighley station on 17 October 1946 with the 1.15pm Oxenhope train to the right, headed by Johnson 0-4-4T No 1275. In Platform 4 is a GN line train from Bradford Exchange via Queensbury worked by ex-GN 'N1' 0-6-2T No 9449.
H. C. Casserley

If you look at one of the basic railway 'tablets of stone', the *Handbook of Stations* issued by the Railway Clearing House, 1904 edition, you will find that Ingrow had a goods yard but that although it was equipped with a five-ton crane it was unable to handle livestock, horseboxes, traction engines or road carriages. Minute Damems was listed as a goods and passenger station but, other than passengers, its staple traffic was milk in churns. Oakworth also had a five-ton crane — it's still there — and livestock could be dealt with. Haworth featured a 10-ton crane but the goods yard did not cater for as full a range of goods traffic as Oxenhope where livestock, horseboxes and prize cattle vans could be accommodated.

Reference to *Bradshaw*, another railway 'bible', shows that on weekdays its April 1910 edition featured 16 trains to Oxenhope, and 19 back to Keighley, with additional midday trains on Saturdays. The majority of trains called at all stations but a handful in each direction (more often downhill) missed out Damems.

Ingrow, with its two stations, one served by the Great Northern via Queensbury and the other on the Worth Valley, was 45-60min from Bradford, the GN trains being on average quicker because after all they provided a through service. One of the endemic disadvantages of the Worth Valley was that for historical reasons the junction with the main line faced towards Skipton, and as such precluded through running from Bradford.

Just before railway Grouping in 1923, the branch passenger service had altered little although there were one or two trains less on weekdays.

Keighley Corporation operated trams as far as Ingrow then, from 1913, it introduced somewhat eccentric trolleybuses on a service between Ingrow and Oxenhope, and then from Keighley to Oakworth. These and later conventional trolleybuses did not survive beyond 1932. In either case, while the roads generally served the valley sides the railway ran along the bottom; in earlier days at least it was more popular for workpeople travelling to their jobs in the mills.

In the interwar period the nature of the branch changed little. Perhaps there was more variety in locomotives with the appearance of 0-6-0 tender engines and, from 1935, the innovation of push-pull working on the branch passenger services, using the Midland 0-4-4Ts that had featured on ordinary trains.

Comparison of the public timetables for 1933 and 1937 reveals little in the way of alterations — 16 or 17 trains to Oxenhope and one or two more back to Keighley, with additional Saturday workings, and six trains each way on Sundays. In-between the passenger service the branch goods took its time getting to Oxenhope and back, shunting in the goods yards en route. On high-days and holidays, excursions were run from Oxenhope to Morecambe or to Blackpool. In return, an increasing number of visitors took the train to Haworth on their way to the Brontë Parsonage.

After World War 2 the well-established routines began to alter. With the onset of war branch passenger services had been trimmed, and by August 1947 there were just nine trains each way on weekdays (12 on Saturdays) and only four trains on Sundays afternoons to Oxenhope and back. In winter, the Sunday service was withdrawn. In May 1949, Damems was closed to traffic and it had to wait until preservation days for its next passenger train.

Based at Skipton shed (Keighley being a sub-shed of Skipton), former Midland Railway locomotives continued to work the branch trains although, from time to time, more modern engines made their appearance. Clearly, the Worth Valley was not being blessed with the cream of motive power. Yet other lines in the locality were being closed, notably the Bradford/Halifax-Keighley passenger service which ceased in May 1955. On better-used lines diesel railcars were introduced. What future was there for the Worth Valley branch?

Rather than abandon the branch British Railways decided to cut operating costs by reducing staff, something that did not happen elsewhere on the system until the 1960s and the onset of Dr Beeching's reforms. The changes occurred late in 1955. All signalboxes were closed and almost all signal-arms removed, the line now being operated under the rules of 'one engine in steam', with staff and key working from Keighley GN Junction signalbox. Ground-frames were installed at Oakworth and Haworth, and these were worked by the only full-time personnel to be employed on the line itself — the crossing-keepers at both these stations.

Station buildings on the branch were taken out of use and redundant sidings lifted. In the place of station booking offices, tickets were issued by the train guard who was equipped with a portable ticket-machine, a familiar feature of more recent years on BR but then unusual. The guard also doubled as a porter at Keighley on weekday mornings.

The steam trains remained but, instead of the compartment stock, there was at least one or more sets of LMS-design centre gangway coaches which had been adapted for push-pull working. These allowed the guard to walk through the train to issue or check tickets. Apart from operating the Worth Valley service, they were also used for some journeys between Bradford and Skipton. In place of the ex-Midland 0-4-4Ts there were now Ivatt designed, BR-built 2-6-2Ts to work the branch passenger trains, although an ex-Midland '3F' 0-6-0 continued in use on the goods service. Except on Saturdays when the goods was out and about on the line there was a morning gap in passenger services between 8.30am and 1.15pm, no doubt dissuading some potential off-peak travellers.

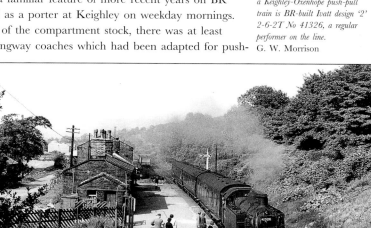

In the meantime, control of the line had passed from the London Midland to the North Eastern Region (NER) which throughout its area pursued a more ruthless policy of cutting uneconomic services. In July 1959, the NER posted notices threatening complete closure of the Oxenhope branch, subject to approval of its proposal by the Transport Users' Consultative Committee (TUCC). Rather than agree to the proposed closure the TUCC instead recommended that the NER should try again, and that train operating costs should be cut by introducing diesel railcars. The NER duly took up the recommendation.

The new service began from 13 June 1960. Although the morning 'gap' remained, between lunchtime and 9pm there was almost an hourly service. Cheap fares were offered such as 1s 2d (6p) for the Keighley-Oxenhope round trip but of course this demonstrated one of the problems: the revenue flow was probably inadequate to cover the direct costs of running the trains. Cheap day returns were needed to attract off-peak travellers from the buses or to make the journeys at all but, as the season ticket-holders anyway enjoyed discounted fares, taken overall the receipts were insufficient. This was despite the fact that over 130,000 passenger journeys were recorded annually on the branch.

At least the NER made a bid to operate an attractive service when, as indeed occurred elsewhere, they might have responded to the TUCC's 'thumbs-down' to its closure proposal by reducing the timetable to a bare minimum. But it was not to last. In what proved to be the final passenger service operated by BR, that beginning in September 1961, the second-class only diesel trains between Keighley and Oxenhope made 15 return journeys on Mondays to Fridays, four more each way on Saturdays but none on Sundays. A note in the timetable proclaimed: 'Cheap Day Return Tickets available by Any Train Any Day are issued between Keighley and Oxenhope and intermediate stations.'

But the NER had already applied again to close the line. This time, despite fierce local opposition, the TUCC complied with its wishes. The last BR passenger trains to Oxenhope and back ran on an almost snowbound Saturday — 30 December 1961 — just 18 months after the diesel railcars had been introduced.

The BR timetable supplement brought out at the 1962 New Year said it all: 'Table 25. Weekdays. The Passenger Train has been withdrawn from Ingrow, Oakworth, Haworth and Oxenhope. *Delete* this Table. Alternative bus services are run by West Yorkshire Road Car Co Ltd and at Keighley by West Yorkshire Services Ltd.'

However, the people of the Worth Valley and its locality were determined that Table 25 would not be *deleted*. The response of local people to news of closure was simple — we'll run the line ourselves. It probably helped that in the meantime the branch freight service continued, and was not scheduled to be withdrawn until June 1962. At least the track would not be torn up overnight.

A century earlier, in the face of the indifference displayed by the Midland Railway and its predecessor, local people had taken it on themselves to proceed with the construction of the railway. Although the Keighley & Worth Valley Railway Co had been dissolved in 1886, most people in the area probably still regarded the single-track to Oxenhope as their railway. Perhaps they knew of families who had subscribed money to the building of the line. Many others used it regularly — it was part of their everyday life. Others might not have travelled on it in recent years but all shared one view. They were sentimentally attached to the line. It was their *railway*.

3: Local People Take Over - Again

Such sentiments were common elsewhere in Britain, and probably apply elsewhere in the world, too. The guiding principle seemed to be that local facilities such as a railway, or indeed other public works, were held in trust for the local community and operated on their behalf. The remote authorities responsible for running the railway — or whatever — could not do as they pleased with it. Those involved in the early 1960s with the campaign to save the Worth Valley's railway are in no doubt of the groundswell of public opinion that assisted them — it's *our* line and if 'they' can't be bothered to run it, then we'll do it ourselves.

First thoughts were that the objective must be to keep the line open, to resist the planned closure. Local opposition had contributed to the TUCC's saying 'no' to BR's closure proposal of 1959. Perhaps closure could be averted again.

Once BR had announced that services would finish at the end of the year, the first moves were made. Ralph Povey, President of the Keighley & Worth Valley Railway Preservation Society today, lived at Oakworth and he wrote a letter to the Bradford *Telegraph and Argus* newspaper which was published in its 15 November 1961 edition.

Previous page:
The first LMS Hughes Fowler 2-6-0, No 2700, was loaned by the National Railway Museum to the K&WVR in its early days. Here it sets out from Keighley with a Santa by Steam working on 14 December 1968.
R. Hodge

Below:
Ready for the off! Keighley's Platform 4 on 21 April 1968 with one of the trial trains operated before the reopening. The engine is Ivatt '2' 2-6-2T No 41241 with former Metropolitan Railway coaches.
Ian G. Holt

Right:
The final BR timetable for the branch.

KEIGHLEY and OXENHOPE
(Diesel Trains) (Second Class Only)

WEEKDAYS ONLY

Stations: KEIGHLEY (dep), Ingrow, Oakworth, Haworth, OXENHOPE (arr)

SO—Saturdays only.   SX—Saturdays excepted.

His letter suggested that a preservation society should be formed to take over the branch line. At that time there were just two standard gauge preserved lines in Britain: the Middleton Railway in Leeds, and the Bluebell Railway in Sussex. The societies supporting both these railway projects had drawn some encouragement from the narrow gauge railways already being run by enthusiasts in Wales.

Ralph Povey had discovered already that there was not much support forthcoming from other railway enthusiasts when it came to preserving his local line. If it was to be saved it would have to be on the basis that local people wanted their line to be kept open for use by the community.

A public meeting was advertised for 24 January 1962, less than a month after BR had withdrawn the passenger service. It had been arranged by a local college lecturer, the late and much missed Bob Cryer. Room 14 in the Keighley Temperance Hall had been booked and that evening it was filled with local people, including business people, enthusiasts and professional railwaymen. The meeting demonstrated genuine enthusiasm and support for the idea that the railway should be taken over and operated by a group of private individuals.

Not untypical of the spirit of that meeting was the proprietor of Clough's Mill, Ingrow who asked: 'Is there going to be a 7.10 in the morning from Oxenhope to get my workers to Ingrow?' As a result of the meeting a committee was set up to work out what might be required to achieve the takeover. Further meetings took place and, on 1 March 1962, a resolution was passed at a public meeting that a preservation society should be formed, to be known as the Keighley and Worth Valley Railway Preservation Society.

Above:
Happily, the K&WVR Preservation Society's first President recorded some of the early developments. Char is being shovelled out of the smokebox of 'Pug' No 51218 at Haworth. Eric Treacy

Above:
Stock begins to arrive — the Gresley Society's 'N2' 0-6-2T arrives at Ingrow on 31 July 1965 with six coaches that have travelled over BR metals to reach the Railway. Next the engine is a ex-LNER corridor brake coach which is owned by the Gresley Society and left the Railway some years ago. Ian G. Holt

Right:
A reminder of the age of some of the vehicles purchased by the VCT from BR service in the mid-1960s. This is an ex-Midland Railway luggage composite coach of 1886, nowadays restored and on display. Robin Higgins

As yet, the principal objective was to offer a regular public passenger service on the line. Ralph Povey explains: 'In the first 12 months we produced mock-up budgets for the railway's operation and they showed income primarily coming from commuter traffic. Income from tourist traffic was only a part of it.' At the time, it was not perhaps apparent that social and travel habits were changing. Having emerged from the privations and restrictions of early postwar years, by the early 1960s car ownership was growing fast. People were moving away from public transport, with inevitable consequences for rail travel: the railways could not continue in their present form.

Above:
Capt Smith's GNR 0-6-0ST No 1247 and the SE&CR-design Continental brake coach in bright, two-tone paintwork, running up and down at Haworth in 1966.
Michael Harris

'Although the Keighley Borough Council did not offer us any money they were supportive in terms of calling local meetings. In those days before the local government reorganisation, after which Keighley and the Worth Valley passed to Bradford's control, everyone knew each other.'

There was clearly enthusiastic local support for the proposed take-over of the line, but were there any dissenting voices? Ralph Povey replies that 'a number of people wrote to the local newspaper to say that we were a bunch of idiots, that our plans would never work, but it was never more than that.'

Through that period it was Bob Cryer who, early Society members such as Graham Mitchell, current Chairman of the Society recalls, 'took us through the wilderness years. Remember it took six years before we began public services. For the first 18 months there was this community feeling, that we would be operating a railway service for the public. It died away, to be replaced by the idea of operating the branch as a preserved railway. There were Richard Greenwood and Robin Higgins and the Lancashire & Yorkshire Railway "Pug", Ian Holt, and pupils from Keighley Grammar School.'

Six names featured in those early days recalls Ralph Povey, including of course Ralph himself: 'There was Bob Cryer, and Hubert Foster, the well-known model engineer and railway photographer accredited by the London Midland & Scottish Railway, not to mention being the author of an influential book on the Settle & Carlisle line. Edgar Chapman had been involved before World War 2 with the Keighley Railway Society although by now this was moribund. Then there was the late John Bellwood (later to be Chief Mechanical Engineer of the National Railway Museum) and also Mike Goodall. The last-named were both professional railwaymen and they had to be careful not to be seen to be involved too deeply. The advice they gave us was essential.'

By the time that the Preservation Society had begun to negotiate with British Railways attitudes were changing, as Ralph Povey comments. 'We had support from the main line railway, BR was prepared to talk to us as rational beings. Although we had talked of taking over the railway, we couldn't afford the purchase price. Bob Cryer was our leading negotiator.' Many of those early committee meetings were held in Bob's kitchen in his house in Providence Lane, Oakworth. Talking of those days, Graham Mitchell reflects: 'We had no money. Bob was our inspiration. He maintained the initiative — his motto was "we can do it". Taking the example of the *Titfield Thunderbolt* it was *our* railway…'.

Ralph Povey continues: 'We dealt with BR's Estates Department at Leeds. Their managers were our main contact although they referred the final deal to London. From talking of outright purchase we moved to an agreed figure of £45,000 with the period of repayment spread over 25 years. What we didn't appreciate at the time was that inflation and interest rates were to work in our favour. Over 25 years of repayment it became easier and easier to make the repayments to BR.'

The line closed to passenger traffic at the end of 1961. From its formation the Preservation Society's committee met monthly but their meetings were open to all members. Having previously held their meetings away from railway property, the next stage was to have a presence on the Worth Valley line itself. From their May 1962 meeting the committee met at Haworth station, courtesy of the station master. Then they asked to rent Haworth station building and it was agreed — the rate was £65 annually plus rates, of course.

A month later, a special train was chartered, to run to Oxenhope and back with the goods engine normally employed on the branch, ex-Midland '3F' 0-6-0 No 43586 at the head of six coaches. Small-ads placed in the railway press advertised 'a special last British Railways passenger train (steam hauled) will be run over the Worth Valley Branch on Saturday afternoon, starting from Bradford (Forster Square). For times and fares, s.a.e.

Below:
Early arrivals at the Railway included small tank engines formerly in industrial use, such as this ex-Manchester Ship Canal 0-6-0T No 31, built by Leeds manufacturer, Hudswell Clarke, which arrived in 1967. It is seen here working the 14.30 Keighley-Oxenhope in the early days of passenger train operations.
Ian G. Holt

please from The Secretary, Keighley & Worth Valley Preservation Society…'. Poor, old 43586 went for scrap later that year. The Club Fixtures section in *Modern Railways* magazine featured the following appeal: 'The Worth Valley Branch…will close to all traffic on 17 June 1962. This most interesting and picturesque line, which runs into the heart of the famous Brontë country, can again operate with your support. Please join your Yorkshire friends…'.

The friends certainly needed help. Society membership at the end of 1962 numbered 266 but, by March 1964, it had fallen to 140. A publicity campaign followed but the total rose to no more than 180 two months later.

Left:
The preservationists were keen to develop their own identity so as to emphasise their independence from BR. A former Metropolitan Railway brake coach purchased from London Transport is being repainted in the Railway's blue and primrose livery at Haworth yard in April 1968. Nowadays it runs in the sombre, but correct all-over brown paintwork of its days with LT.
Ian G. Holt

Below:
Society members get to grips with the steam dome of 2-6-2T No 41241 in this May 1967 picture.
Ian Bentley

Below:
Reopening day, 29 June 1968. This was the triumphal scene when the inaugural public train arrived at Oxenhope. Leading is Ivatt tank No 41241, behind which is the USA tank No 72. Less obvious are the two Union Jacks carried above No 41241's bufferbeam.
D. N. Scott

Inset:
The Railway settles down to its new existence: on the second day of services 0-6-0T No 72 heads through the peaceful, rural valley towards Oxenhope with a train from Keighley on 30 June 1968.
Ian G. Holt

Behind the scenes Bob Cryer and colleagues were negotiating with BR and, by September 1964, an agreement with BR had been drawn-up. By the end of that year the Society had 223 members. Less than a year later there were 653 and the first visible signs of the Society's success were apparent: rolling stock had begun to arrive in Haworth yard. The station building at Haworth was opened on Sunday afternoons so that visitors could inspect a collection of railway relics.

At the 1965 Spring Bank Holiday, the Society held an Open Day at Haworth and ex-Lancashire & Yorkshire 'Pug' 0-4-0ST No 51218 was in steam in the goods yard. This engine had arrived earlier that year. One comment from those days is 'The Rochdale faction with their "Pug" dominated the Railway'.

Captain W. G. Smith offered to loan his Great Northern Railway 0-6-0ST No 1247, and in March 1965 this engine took up to Haworth the first rolling stock to arrive at Haworth by rail. One of the visitors was your author. Like others he watched as No 1247 trundled along the siding at Haworth during 1966 with a former South Eastern & Chatham Railway coach built for Continental boat trains, and now gaudy in primrose-yellow and blue paintwork. Then it was just another piece of rolling stock. Today it sits beautifully restored in Southern Railway livery and protected in the Vintage Carriages Trust's museum at Ingrow.

Below:
A reminder that the reopening of the line overlapped the end of main line steam. On 3 August 1968, to mark the end of everyday steam working on BR that weekend, No 41241 carries a Farewell to Steam headboard.
Derek Cross

Ralph Povey recalls the atmosphere of 1965. 'We had No 1247 and the Chatham brake coach. We thought we were railwaymen. Give the people a ride and raise money for ourselves. The emphasis was on getting funds together for there was no rich benefactor behind us. A jumble sale made £14 and we were delighted. Robin Higgins organised railway pencils and cards as a way of bringing-in revenue. And the Brontës and Haworth did us no harm at all!'

'The other day someone said to me, "Ralph, what was it like in the *heady* days?" My answer was that we weren't aware that they *were* the heady days. We just ploughed on. We had an idea and we set out to make it work.'

Progress was often agonisingly slow. Tools, expertise and experience were in short supply. Agreement was reached for the Society to lease Platform 4 at Keighley station which with Platform 3 was in danger at one stage of being pulled down by BR. David Pearson, now a Vice-Chairman of the Society but then a schoolboy, recalls going to BR Keighley's station master for the keys to open-up Platform 4.

A lot of work had to be carried out at all the stations before public services could be operated, and to provide servicing facilities for engines and stabling for stock. The dismantling of the former GN line to Ingrow released material for reuse on the Worth Valley line. Over the last few years of BR operation the line's assets had been reduced to the minimum, and it had ceased to be self-contained. All this had to be rectified.

With steam age BR still all around the preservationists, the Society wanted to establish its own image. In its early days the Railway was a magnet for many locomotives and coaches which though charming in their own right were not suitable for running regular services. Until the new owners of the Worth Valley's railway actually began to run trains the idea was that there would be commuter trains on weekdays worked by diesel railbuses and steam-operated tourist trains at weekends and holidays. But a year-round service demanded full-time paid staff and that was clearly out of the question. A Light Railway Order had also to be obtained before the Society could run trains in its own right.

When the first season's timetable was being planned in 1968 the idea was that the two diesel railbuses would work in the mornings, steam-hauled tourist trains taking over in the afternoons. That is what happened.

Opposite:
It's difficult to believe now but Oakworth station was not fully restored from the word go! It looks trim enough in this January 1969 as Peckett 0-4-0ST No 1999 calls with a Haworth-bound train. This engine was formerly used as a gasworks shunter by North West Gas Board.
N. Hellewell

Below:
One of the German-built, ex-BR railbuses departs from Haworth with an Oxenhope train in February 1969.
N. A. Hunt

The irony was that the intended launch of services on the new Keighley & Worth Valley took place during a summer of discontent on British Rail. Trial trains to simulate regular operations began running in the spring of 1968. On the appointed day of reopening, 29 June 1968, no trains ran at all on BR at the culmination of a work-to-rule campaign by the rail unions. That first public service train was hauled by Ivatt Class 2 2-6-2T No 41241, painted in crimson-lake livery and proudly lettered K&WVR, and US-built 0-6-0T No 30072, in a cheery golden-brown paint scheme with silver-painted smokebox door.

First President of the K&WVR until his untimely death in 1978, the late Bishop Eric Treacy, described the day's scene so well: 'And what a picture they [the engines] made thundering up the Worth Valley. It had all the atmosphere of a great occasion, with photographers galore chasing the train up the valley, crowds of people at all vantage points up the line and a prize silver band to serenade the engines. Nearly as much steam was used blowing the engine whistles that day as to propel the train. For the locals this was more than the job of pulling a few coaches five miles up the valley — it was a triumph for private and local enterprise over a monolithic central authority which had closed their line.'

Below right:
Oxenhope station was somewhat forlorn when the Society took over. Among the early installations was this makeshift but necessary water tank supported by concrete sleepers. It appears in a September 1969 scene of the USA tank waiting to leave with a Keighley train.
P. R. Foster

Below:
By September 1969, the date of this picture, much had been done to spruce up that part of Keighley station used by the Worth Valley. A public address system had been installed and hanging baskets helped to brighten the scene.
Colin Boocock

Below:
A happily posed picture dating from February 1969 which was a notably snowy month. North Eastern Railway-design Class J72 0-6-0T No 69023 Joem crosses Mytholmes Viaduct, bound for Haworth and Oxenhope.
R. I. Vallance

Well, it had to appear, didn't it? Of all the filming assignments or tv commercials that have involved preserved lines, the most memorable was the use of the K&WVR's LMS 'Black Five' No 5212 in advertising material produced by a wallpaper paste manufacturer. With Class 'A' headlamps the 'Five' pauses with a train at Oakworth station. K&WVR

The *Railway World* of August 1968 was a commemorative issue of the magazine to mark the End of BR Steam. Among the regrets and the prospects for an uncertain future was a report on the rebirth of the Keighley & Worth Valley Railway.

The journal informed readers: 'For the remainder of the summer season the line will operate each Saturday and Sunday with steam traction on most trains although two diesel railbuses and a diesel locomotive are also available for certain services.' It went on to remind readers that 'The K&WVR is the second standard gauge passenger line to be operated by a privately-owned company supported by a preservation society.'

To return to Eric Treacy and to what he wrote in Ian Allan's *Steam Alive!* in the summer of 1969:

'At the top of the cobbled hill is Haworth Parish Church and the Parsonage, which is now the Brontë Museum. At the bottom of the hill is Haworth station, now in the ownership of the Keighley & Worth Valley Preservation Society. You can take your choice — if you have literary leanings, go up the hill. If you incline to railway relics — locomotives, carriages, and other bits of precious old iron, then stay at the bottom of the hill.

'At the bottom of the hill, you will find a rich variety of locomotives, in the station buildings a "tuck" shop, a bookshop and a museum of railwayana. Every weekend you will find a number of pilgrims who have come from all parts of England to potter round the yards. And you will find various members of the Society, all absorbed in the multitudinous tasks that arise in the running of a railway by volunteers. In the workshop the fitters will be hard at it — the painters will be busy putting new colours on to old engines; members, in a variety of uniforms, will be acting as porters, guards, and car park attendants, while a small but very select group will be driving and firing the locomotives. Among these volunteers will be a number of professional railwaymen, taking their time off "messing about with steam".'

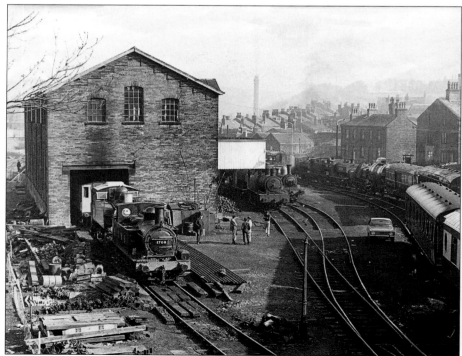

Right:
Somehow this sort of image of Haworth yard is rooted firmly in many people's minds although numerous changes have been made since this April 1969 view. Nearest is ex-Midland '1F' 0-6-0T No 1708 which most recently revisited the Railway in the autumn of 1997. Just visible is the smoke rising from Joem which is being steamed for the day's work. Note that the coaching stock is also being stabled in the yard.
Peter Milburn

He continued:

'If one had to trace all this enthusiasm to its source, I believe one would find that the motive power came from Bob Cryer, a technical college lecturer, who is Chairman of the Society and who has from the outset believed it possible to run this railway efficiently with a group of enthusiasts. In this belief he has never wavered and, with an admirable blend of firmness and humour, has piloted the Society through a succession of problems to its present active existence.'

Inset:
A charming picture of the days when the public were given rides on industrial (more precisely, former railway contractors') engines in Ingrow yard. This was during a Steam Gala Weekend. On the left of the picture is the diminutive Hudswell Clarke 0-4-0ST Lord Mayor *of 1893, with Manning Wardle* Sir Berkeley *(built 1891) to the right.*
Rodney Wildsmith

Below:
Steaming into the 1970s — a Sunday shuttle from Haworth approaches Oxenhope on 4 January 1970, with USA tank No 72 at the head of a BR Standard non-gangwayed open second and the SE&CR-design Continental brake.
John M. Boyes

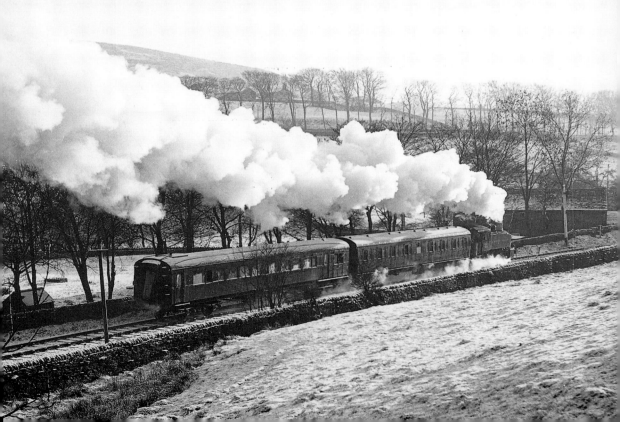

Eric Treacy brings our chapter to an appropriate conclusion: '...the result is a classless and united Society in which differences in social background, education, religion, politics and income are submerged in the common task of showing that in this part of Yorkshire there exists a group of "tykes" who, having put their hands to the plough, are determined not to look back.'

What was a good observation in 1969 is as true a verdict on the Keighley & Worth Valley almost 30 years later.

Right:
As services developed after 1968, a number of alterations were necessary to improve train working: initial attempts to offer augmented services at public holidays proved chaotic, and to overcome this a loop was put in just south of Damems in 1971. Work was well in hand when LMS 'Black Five' No 5025 passed with an Oxenhope train on 2 May that year. This engine was loaned to the K&WVR until the Strathspey Railway was able to accept it.
Robin Higgins

Below:
The main part of Keighley Platform 4 looked attractive but an extension was needed both to this platform and to No 3 to accommodate longer trains. Note the state of the track. When photographed on 7 August 1970, the two railbuses were on their way on to BR metals, to turn on the triangle at Shipley.
Robin Higgins

Right:
The existing headshunt at Oxenhope (although extended by the Society) was not long enough for some of the larger engines or when trains were double-headed. Here it is in the process of being lengthened during May 1971.
Robin Higgins

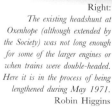

T he decade following the reopening of the Worth Valley's railway saw operations develop very gradually as it took some time for resources to be increased to effect radical changes and so permit progress beyond the immediate task of creating a safe, reliable and passenger-friendly undertaking. The period got off to an excellent start with a marvellous publicity boost in the form of EMI's full-length feature film, The Railway Children, which was released at Christmas 1970. While the Railway carried nearly 71,000 passengers in 1970 the effect of the film was that carryings soared to over 125,000 in 1971. Subsequently, they fell back, but then rose steadily.

4: Towards Maturity

Facilities for locomotive servicing and carriage stabling were improved during the early and mid-1970s. So were the stations and, although the others had to be altered somewhat to cater for more traffic than they had probably seen at any time in their existence, Oakworth could be maintained as a country wayside station, and indeed remains so today. The station was entered in the first Best Preserved Railway Station Competition staged in 1979 (now incorporated in the Ian Allan National Railway Heritage Awards) and was adjudged the outright winner. Writing about the judges' choice of Oakworth, railway historian, Gordon Biddle commented: '…the standard of workmanship and maintenance…was first-class and the degree of authenticity virtually impeccable.'

Much more might be said about the K&WVR during the 1970s but perhaps it is best summed-up by the success with Oakworth station. In time, and particularly during the

1980s, the other stations were transformed to sit comfortably with the standards set by Oakworth.

While the stations were in the public eye, the Railway's civil engineers also had to draw-up a programme of renewals for the trackwork and structures, there being 31 bridges, tunnels and culverts in the line's 4¾ miles. The bridges in particular had to receive special attention as the previous owners had allowed a backlog of maintenance to form.

Other developments included the provision of Pullman standard on-train catering with the restoration of Pullman Car No 84, renamed *Mary* and an attendant bar car. We need to move further ahead in the story to see how covered facilities, time and expertise were able to improve the condition of the other passenger stock. Writing in the railway press during 1983 Mike Symm pointed out: 'Of the groups of volunteer workers on the Railway, by far the smallest is the Carriage and Wagon Department. Only a handful of people regularly turn up to restore, maintain and clean the Railway's fleet of 16 coaches used in regular traffic.'

But things were changing and Mike Symm was able to report spectacular progress on the restoration of some important vehicles, the biggest collection of historic coaches on the Railway belonging to the Vintage Carriages Trust.

During the 1970s although there were some notable successes, the provision of motive power to work the trains was often a struggle and the Society was sometimes hard-pressed to keep engines serviceable. In April 1980, Southern Bulleid Pacific No 34092 *City of Wells* was returned to service from scrap condition, and other locomotives returned to traffic that same year were the Ivatt Class 2 2-6-2T No 41241 and ex-Lancashire & Yorkshire Railway 0-6-0ST No 752. The summer 1981 services were worked by five engines: No 41241, three engines that had been rescued from Woodhams', Barry scrapyard and over the years returned to service at Haworth — LMS-design '8F' 2-8-0 No 8431, BR '4' 4-6-0 No 75078 and Midland '4F' 0-6-0 No 43924 — and *Big Jim*, the US-built 2-8-0 No 5820 from World War 2 which had been obtained from Poland.

The Railway had seen a steady growth in traffic during the late 1970s and special events such as the Enthusiasts' Weekend, which it can be said to have invented, went from strength to strength. For 1980, a press release going to the railway press promised that 'a busy season is expected and fares reductions of up to 10p will be offered until the end of May'. During the summer of 1980, however, fares had to rise by 10%, despite a record level of traffic because, said the Railway, it had faced increased costs of more than 20% in recent months. Yet 1981 saw more than 150,000 passengers carried, despite unpromising economic conditions.

A weekend visit to the line early in 1984 led the author to comment that 'the K&WVRPS has established a mature railway and created a public institution. What the pioneers were driving at has become accepted and enjoyed by the public at large.' One of the Railway's leading-lights wondered about possible future problems of stagnation, but although the line could not be physically extended there was another way to widen its appeal. The example lay in Oakworth station — attract more people because the Railway was able to offer the very best in standards in trains, stations and presentation. The Society had come to appreciate that 'the authentic railway sells'.

Also, the attitude towards preserved railways was changing, They had the potential for providing more than a train ride from A to B and back again. Instead, it was becoming clear that the K&WVR could offer a complete experience. Running from a town through industry and into countryside, it has a charming variety of stations, a tunnel and a viaduct (or two). The locomotive depot had plenty of space for visitors. The Railway was able to turn out a good variety of motive power.

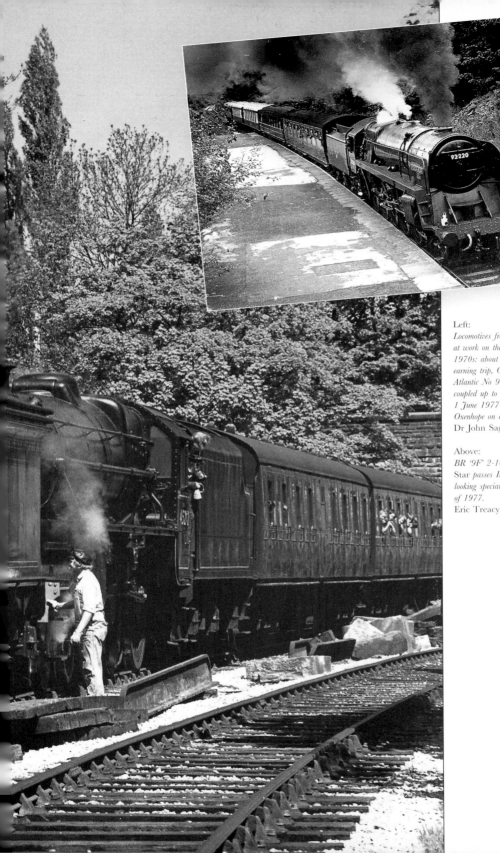

Left:
Locomotives from the National Collection at work on the Worth Valley in the 1970s: about to make its first revenue-earning trip, Great Northern Railway Atlantic No 990 Henry Oakley *is coupled up to 'Black Five' No 45212 on 1 June 1977 to work as pilot to Oxenhope on a schoolchildren's excursion.*
Dr John Sagar

Above:
BR '9F' 2-10-0 No 92220 Evening Star *passes Ingrow with a prestigious-looking special in the early autumn of 1977.*
Eric Treacy

WORTH VALLEY RAILWAY
1968-1978

There was already a focal point in the Worth Valley with the attractions and historical associations of Haworth Village but, by the early/mid-1980s, the Railway had stimulated a more general and creative interest in the past. People were coming out for the day to travel on the Railway and to take in other attractions. Some visitors indeed imagined a more direct link-up between the K&WVR and the erstwhile inhabitants of Haworth Parsonage: 'Where do we take the steam train for the Brontes?' was not an unusual request at Haworth.

During the mid-1980s, the concept of railway preservation was beginning to widen beyond the business of running trains. An interest in gas lighting came from close association with the same, seeing that Oakworth station was still innocent of an electricity supply (and other stations are also gas-lit) and, in pursuit of authenticity, working gas lamp standards were installed in the yard of the upgraded Oxenhope station. Nowadays the K&WVR claims to be Britain's third largest public gas lighting utility.

Having mentioned stations, compared with some other preserved railways of the time it was fair to say that those on the K&WVR were of a consistently high standard — and getting better.

At Keighley, Platforms 3/4 used by the Railway had been restored to the London Midland Region style of the 1950s. Where steel frameless signs could not be obtained, hand-painted wooden replacements were substituted. The K&WVR ticket office was formerly a sweet kiosk at Manchester Central station; along with the ex-Lancashire & Yorkshire Railway departure clock and the buffet, the overall effect was — and is indeed today — of a bustling station with plenty of space for passengers. One particularly good feature which has been maintained at this and other K&WVR stations is the clear provision of train information to passengers, usually in the form of attractive 1950s-style posters.

By the early 1980s it was becoming clear that stations could absorb money in unnoticed ways, quite apart from the dry-rot at Oakworth. The smokeplates installed on Keighley's underbridge in 1984 cost a cool £10,000. One of the acknowledged weaknesses at Keighley at the time was the lack of signalling and it is taking some time to rectify this. One attractive feature of recent years was the installation in 1990 of the Midland Railway turntable formerly at Garsdale.

Ingrow West tended not to be mentioned in the Railway's guidebooks, for some station buildings had been demolished, and thereafter it became an unstaffed halt which was characterised by vandalism. In 1985, there was a vision of better things for Ingrow. The Railway had been offered the derelict station buildings at Foulridge on the former Midland Railway Colne-Skipton line for just £7,500 and there was free labour to move and rebuild them. But other costs and materials had to be considered and the final bill promised to be £50,000. An appeal was launched in the Preservation Society's magazine *Push and Pull* and, although some donations came in, clearly they would not be enough.

A few days later, current K&WVR Vice-Chairman, David Pearson, received a phone-call from a remarkable man, T. Geoffrey Reeday Llb (Hons) (Lond) FCIS, ACIB, Hon FCIB, of Lincoln's Inn. He offered to underwrite the whole project of moving the buildings at Foulridge to Ingrow, casually enquiring, 'It won't cost more than £100,000, will it?' Mr Reeday made it clear that David and his colleagues should just get on with the project — it was *his* job to worry about the funding.

The station at Ingrow was effectively recreated, but better than ever before, and dedicated to the memory of Geoffrey's father who had been born nearby in 1890. The rebuilt station was rededicated on 22 July 1989 at a ceremony presided over by the Lord-Lieutenant for West Yorkshire, The Lord Ingrow OBE TD. Geoffrey Reeday died in October 1997 but his generosity has assured him and his father of a lasting and marvellous memorial.

Inset:
1978 was a bitter-sweet year for the Society. In the May there was great sadness at the death of its President, the Rt Rev Eric Treacy. The Provost of Bradford led the Service of Remembrance in Haworth loco yard on 2 September 1978.
Dr John Sagar

Left:
In late June the 10th anniversary of reopening was commemorated, not least by the working of this special train headed by the USA tank which had been converted as an oil-burner in 1976. The date is 24 June 1978 and the train is seen on the approach to Haworth.
Dr John Sagar

news about **Steam Trains**
ON THE KEIGHLEY AND WORTH VALLEY LIGHT RAILWAY
(Yorkshire's steam railway)

Above:
By the late 1970s the Railway was becoming adept at promoting itself: press releases appeared on headed paper defiantly proclaiming Yorkshire's steam railway…

Right:
In due course, there was justifiable pride at the operation of what was described as the 'only railway buffet car in the world to sell real ale…'. Yes, you could get keg elsewhere, but the dig was also directed at BR whose new HSTs were originally supposed to serve keg beer but it all ended up as a horrible mistake. The K&WVR never looked back with on-train beer. K&WVR

Below right:
Much later, in 1985, the K&WVR made an excellent job of resurrecting a very down-at-heel BR dining car (one of the oldest Mk 1s) to provide a very adequate saloon with 2+2 seating. K&WVR

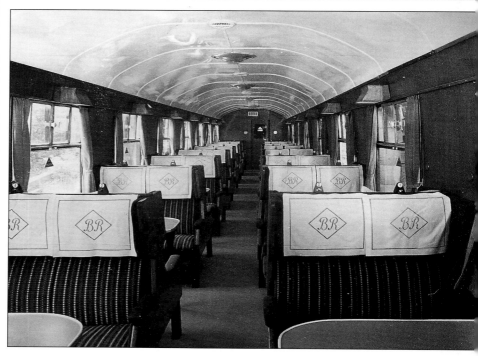

Damems is a delight. It was probably one of the smallest stations in the country (emphatically not a halt, these usually being unstaffed), and as late as 1947 had retained a station master. The station group includes a level crossing and 1923-vintage crossing keeper's house. To this has been added a signalbox removed from Earby, later had to be replaced by a replica as it had succumbed to rot. In addition to the signalbox, the booking office is also a transplant, and originally served as the goods checker's office in Keighley station yard. The booking office of this delightful station was commissioned in April 1984 and subsequently the station has been further titivated and improved.

Oakworth station had already become something of a legend by the 1980s, not least for its regular appearance among the winners of the Best Restored Station Competition. Unfortunately, during the autumn of 1983, an outbreak of dry-rot was discovered in the entrance hall. Woodwork and plaster had to be hacked out and replaced, and professional repairs carried out to the roof. After the remedial attention, the framed portrait of Queen Victoria was securely back in its place over the fireplace and generally the station looked as if it had remained untouched and unspoiled.

Haworth station has changed relatively little over the years apart from landscaping on the 'other' side of the track to the platform. One of its most notable features is the lattice footbridge over the line at the south end of the station.

Oxenhope station was greatly enhanced during the 1970s and early 1980s. It was the subject of a major improvement scheme undertaken by the Railway in concert with Bradford Metropolitan District Council. One result was a much-needed stone-setted 'street' the whole length of the station yard. Properly marked-out car parking spaces were provided, as well as a bus standing area. Overall, the station yard area was tidied up and properly paved whilst gas lamps added the final touch.

Other major engineering projects were carried out at Haworth locomotive depot, involving construction of a new shed and a purpose-built volunteers' hostel.

One aspect of the early 1980s was the attempt to develop public transport access to the Railway, some preserved railways tending to be rather too reliant on car-borne visitors. No less than 30% of passengers were arriving at the K&WVR by public transport and, on some days, 50% of traffic at Keighley was generated by rail.

Made as Good as New...

Inset:
The 101th engine to be recovered from Woodhams, Barry scrapyard was 1924-built LMS '3F' 0-6-0T No 47279 which arrived at Haworth during 1979 and is seen here in typical ex-Barry state in March 1980. The K&WVR was home to the very first Barry escapee which was '4F' 0-6-0 No 43924.
Peter Harris

Below:
No 47279, eight years later, on 28 February 1988, having had a steam test following restoration to working order. Its companions are Bellerophon (to its left) and visiting GWR pannier tank No 7752, based at the Birmingham Railway Museum. Behind the engines is the newish running shed.
D. Stuart Lindsey

The K&WVR and the West Yorkshire Passenger Transport Executive of the time worked hard to make it generally known that the Railway was regarded as part of West Yorkshire's public transport network. Although bus services have been subjected to major change over the last few years, something of this approach remains.

Another feature of the early 1980s which has been developed further is the use of vintage buses on services connecting with the Railway, thereby extending the appeal of the visit as an all-round transport day out. Nowadays the buses are usually provided courtesy of Keighley Bus Museum, as Chapter 5 describes. Railway road vehicles are also being operated as another complementary attraction; again, these feature in Chapter 5.

At Ingrow, the Vintage Carriages Trust has established its museum and workshops for the display, maintenance and restoration of its priceless collection of locomotives and vintage rolling stock. Attention to its stock had previously been carried out at Oxenhope but during the 1980s it was decided to relocate to Ingrow where a carriage shed would be built so that work could continue uninterrupted. With financial support from various authorities and more than 800 individuals, the Ingrow Carriage Museum was opened in 1990. A substantial extension was completed in 1997 and formally opened in May 1998. Deservedly, the VCT received the Association of Railway Preservation Societies Annual Award in 1990 for the creation of the Museum, and the associated transformation of Ingrow goods yard.

During 1990, the Railway was strengthened by the arrival of the Bahamas Locomotive Society from its former base at Dinting, near Manchester. The Society moved in to Ingrow station yard, where a workshop, museum and sidings are being developed using the former goods shed as a base. Coming with the Society was the fine LNWR 'Coal Tank' No 1054 in its care. Built in 1888, this engine is a real gem and had already established a devoted following. Its arrival perhaps encouraged the traditionalists.

Earlier the comment was made that, by the early 1980s, the Railway had come to appreciate that 'the authentic railway sells'. A decade later, the typical Worth Valley train comprised a smart, modern steam loco at the head of Mk 1 coaches, also clean and smart, the ensemble dating from the 1950s or 1960s. Nothing wrong about that but how

Inset:
Over Here…
The US-built 'S160' class 2-8-0 built for service in World War 2 came to the K&WVR from Poland. Soon after arrival it was prepared for service and is seen here on its very first run on the line, painted in Polish State Railways' livery as Tr 203 474. Alongside at Keighley, '4F' No 43924 seems to be wearing a rather knowing expression. The final batch of '4Fs' entered service on the LMS just a few years before the 2-8-0 was built.
Rodney Wildsmith

Opposite:
Back Here…
A British wartime engine which first saw service in the Netherlands, and then was sold to Swedish State Railways which in turn released it to the K&WVR in 1973. The engine was use for a few years only (it is seen here in largely Swedish condition, departing from Keighley in August 1977) and has been undergoing overhaul and rebuilding since 1990. It will be outshopped as a BR engine and should enter traffic for the millennium.
John Cooper-Smith

Left:
A splendid spectacle as, with flags flying and with 'Golden Arrow' insignia in place, newly restored Bulleid Pacific No 34092 City of Wells departs Keighley for Oxenhope on its first ceremonial run after 'renaming' on 1 April 1980.
Dr John Sagar

come that the preservation society which was formed early enough to acquire some really vintage engines and coaches was hard-pressed, despite the sterling efforts of the Vintage Carriages Trust, to turn out a serviceable Victorian train? Also, how was it that the said vintage stock was languishing in limbo in various sheds when it might have been working? Not only that but, until at least the mid-1950s, the typical Keighley-Oxenhope passenger train was very much a pre-Grouping train, yet the preservationists could not apparently field one for the 1990s.

Reverting to Type.
Below:
Having carried K&WVR livery since 1968, when outshopped in March 1980 the Ivatt 2-6-2T appeared in BR lined black livery, here being applied at Oxenhope.
Dr John Sagar

Right:
The USA tank similarly returned to a livery it had worn in BR days when it was converted back as a coal burner, and passed for limited main line operations in late 1987. As No 30072 it is seen at Haworth running shed at the time, carrying its memorably luminous version of BR malachite-green livery.
D. Stuart Lindsey

A catalyst was needed. During 1993, which marked the 25th anniversary of the line's reopening, Handel Kardas, the then Editor of *Railway World* magazine, was invited to provide the K&WVR with an appraisal and he was urged to be honest — give us a verdict in your article, they said, warts and all. Most of his comments were congratulatory, apart from strictures about the downbeat aspect of entrance to the Railway's part of Keighley station and the unappealing engineers' yard at otherwise exemplary Oakworth.

However, Handel reserved his main criticism for the policy on locomotives and rolling stock for he commented, ' …this is the real tragedy of the Worth Valley; that its comprehensive collection of stock is not being used to its fullest advantage'. He went on to say, '…for the line to be *complete* it needs the older relics in use, as much as it needs its older locos'.

Commenting that the arrival from Dinting of the London & North Western Railway 'Coal Tank' and its use on Worth Valley trains had attracted considerable interest, he said that '…(it) should surely have sparked off interest in the Lancashire & Yorkshire 0-6-0 and 0-6-0ST, the "Pugs" and the genuine Midland Railway "4F", or hastened the overhaul of the Taff Vale 0-6-2T.'

Although some feathers were ruffled by Handel's observations, someone *was* listening and the last few years have seen progress 'hastening' on all these fronts. At the time of his article's appearance in late 1993, the Keighley & Worth Valley Trust had recently been set up, with the object of gilding the lily by improving the authenticity of the Railway's operations. As it happened, the K&WVR was home to the largest collection of stock from the Lancashire & Yorkshire Railway, with three locomotives and four coaches in the care of the L&YR Preservation Society.

Below:
Nearing Oxenhope the railway seems to be running through parkland, an impression emphasised in this April 1984 study of the LMS '8F' working to Oxenhope with an Enthusiasts' Day train. At this stage, it was painted as LMS No 8431.
W. A. Sharman

Above right:
The 1980s saw the Railway take especial care to re-create the style of BR's London Midland Region of the 1950s at all but one of its stations. Seen here, a between-workings view of the Ivatt tank and an ex-LMS bogie brake van, with BR signage and posters.
Terry Hanson

Right:
Damems in the 80s — small but good.
Dr John Sagar

Left:
Support from local authorities allowed Oxenhope station's environs to be paved and tidied-up. At the time, this Bedford OB coach was used on a vintage bus service. Such workings are nowadays a regular feature of the Railway's special events.
Dr John Sagar

Top left:
Oakworth preserves the atmosphere of a pre-Grouping station: a coal fire burns brightly, as does the gas mantle.
K&WVR

Top right:
Outside, the lamplighter gets to work…
Brian Dobbs

Below:
Oakworth goods shed is the setting for this attractive March 1988 shot of Haydock Foundry 0-6-0WT Bellerophon.
Brian Dobbs

An idea began to take shape by which the Keighley & Worth Valley Trust and its sister organisations would create the only complete, single company pre-Grouping train in the country. This would represent a four-coach passenger train of the old L&YR, such as might have been in use on the Isle of Axholme Joint Railway some time after 1900.

On the K&WVR was an L&YR 0-6-0 dating from 1887, 'Ironclad' No 957, which had been purchased by Tony Cox in 1959. The engine had seen limited service on the Railway, and notably as *The Green Dragon*, a star performer in the making of *The Railway Children* motion picture, but in 1975 it was retired to become a static exhibit at Oxenhope.

Some years ago, the Railway began to discuss the engine's future with its owner and, following the emergence of the Keighley & Worth Valley Trust, a plan began to be drawn up for No 957's acquisition. Bradford businessman, Roger Bowers now arrived on the scene and agreed to meet the purchase price, with the engine's ownership being transferred to the Bowers 957 Trust.

Worth Valley Diesels.
Opposite below:
*Experimental 'English Electric'
500hp diesel-electric shunter
No D226* Vulcan *has earned
its keep since arriving on the line
in 1966. During the snowstorms
of December 1990 it brings a
Santa Special into Keighley.*
D. Stuart Lindsey

Left:
*BR Class 31/4 diesel
No 31444 was named*
Keighley & Worth Valley
Railway *on 17 August 1988.
It worked to Oxenhope and back
with a special for invited guests.
This is seen departing Keighley
where the naming ceremony had
just taken place.*
John B. Gosling

Below:
*Special diesel enthusiast weekends
have not featured regularly in
recent years. Looking somewhat
out of place, 'Deltic' No 55016*
Gordon Highlander, *at that
time based on the Nene Valley
Railway, leaves Haworth
with a Keighley train on
5 November 1988.*
Les Nixon

The total cost of the 957 Project will be at least £130,000, of which some £75,000 have been raised. The 111-year-old engine is now undergoing overhaul at Bridgnorth on the Severn Valley Railway, and is due to be running on the K&WVR before the millennium.

Meanwhile, funding from the Heritage Lottery Fund has made it possible for the L&YR Preservation Society to progress with the overhaul of another vintage L&YR engine, 0-6-0ST No 752. This was built in 1881 as an 0-6-0 tender engine but later rebuilt as a yard shunter. No 752 is in the process of overhaul, principally at Haworth. The L&YRPS's L&YR 0-4-0ST, BR No 51218, was overhauled at Bury in 1997 and is now back in action on its home line, delighting enthusiasts as it bustles along on demonstration goods trains and undertakes shunting in Ingrow yard.

Work is progressing on the L&YR coaches which will form the celebrity train. Already on hand is the splendidly restored L&YR brake third vehicle which dates from 1910 but its three intended companions are still being worked upon. They include two conventional six-wheelers and also something exceptional, the onetime Club Coach which was built for use by businessmen on their residential trips between Blackpool and Manchester. Its body was sold-off for use as a sports pavilion many years ago but had survived largely intact and has now been matched with a suitable underframe. Restoration is progressing well at Oxenhope, thanks to generous funding from Roger Bowers who has helped the 957 Project to get under way.

Right:
One inspired project has seen the reconstruction at Ingrow station of the Midland Railway station buildings from Foulridge: the platform side of the building, seen in July 1990.
Nigel Hunt

Below:
A plaque in the booking hall commemorates the reconstruction of the station. On the left of this picture of the July 1989 unveiling ceremony is the K&WVRPS Chairman, Graham Mitchell; on the right is The Lord Ingrow.
Dr John Sagar

Inset opposite:
Another achievement in the last decade was the removal from Garsdale and its subsequent re-erection at Keighley of an almost legendary turntable. Garsdale (originally Hawes Junction) turntable was stockaded, to prevent it from spinning round during gales, as was claimed once to have occurred.
Real Photographs (K2084)

Opposite:
North Eastern Railway 'P3' 0-6-0 No 2392, owned by the North Eastern Locomotive Preservation Society and visiting the Worth Valley, poses on the newly installed turntable at Keighley on 18 August 1990.
Dr John Sagar

Apart from progress with the L&YR train, another exceptional pre-Grouping engine is nearing the end of a nine-year restoration to take it from a definitely inactive state to a working engine in its original condition. This is Taff Vale Railway 0-6-2T No 85, built in 1899, which is likely to be steamed very shortly, for the first time in 30 years.

One of the K&WVR's greatest strengths has been mentioned already — its people. The Railway is distinctive for its freedom from damaging internal dissensions of the kind experienced over the years by some railways with an operating company at odds with volunteers forming the supporting preservation society. One reason has been the freedom from Management with a capital 'M'. The structure of control has sometimes been reasonably described as 'something like a workers' co-operative'. 'Everything is discussed in committees whose officers must present minutes and decisions to the Council — it's much like the old local authority system of committees', has been the explanation. 'There are plenty of good debates, but no disputes, even if we spend endless time in committee deliberations'. There is no general manager, no board, no supernumerary management on the K&WVR — and small chance of the disputes known on other preserved railways when Management Moves in Mysterious Ways, contrary to the wishes of volunteers.

Below:
During 1990, the Bahamas Locomotive Society relocated from Dinting and the Vintage Carriages Trust's museum was opened at Ingrow. Tracklaying is in progress in Ingrow goods yard while in the background the VCT museum is prominent. Meanwhile, 'Jubilee' No 45596 Bahamas *passes with a service train.*
Dr John Sagar

Above:
Major changes have occurred recently with the opening of an extension to the VCT's Ingrow museum. Another feature is the paving of the goods yard at this station. The 'Coal Tank' waits for the road' at the exit from Ingrow yard in April 1998 with ex-Met brake coach LT No 427.
Handel Kardas

Left:
VCT craftsman have rebuilt the fire-damaged brake end of ex-GNR coach No 2856 which is currently being extensively restored. As seen in April 1998.
Handel Kardas

The system is certainly a model of democracy, and notable as there are no meetings behind closed doors — any Society member can attend Council meetings. The Worth Valley's style of democratic decision-making manages to give subjects requiring decision the chance of thorough discussion. As in the early days of the Railway there has always been a strong vein of Yorkshire commonsense. The strong local representation has much to do with good communication between Society officers and there are close social bonds.

In true Yorkshire fashion, and a characteristic which led to the line being 'saved' in the first place, once roused the K&WVR is a formidable defender of its hard-won success. It rounded impressively and accurately on the attempts to create a ratepayers' preserved railway in the Spen Valley, and others in the 'professional' heritage railway movement have learned not to tangle with the Railway.

The Keighley & Worth Valley Railway and its operation

The K&WVR Co Ltd: (the legal mouthpiece of the Society):

Ten directors. Chairman: Graham Mitchell. Meet bi-monthly. 90% of shares held by two nominees of the Society.

The K&WVR Preservation Society:

Annual General Meeting elects by vote Society officers and 18 members of Council for the ensuing year. Council meets monthly. Eleven Committees covering all aspects of operation meet regularly and report to the Council.

KEIGHLEY & WORTH VALLEY RAILWAY

News Release

WORTH VALLEY

THE
KEIGHLEY & WORTH VALLEY
RAILWAY
PRESERVATION SOCIETY

The Railway Station
Haworth
Keighley
West Yorkshire BD22 8NJ
Telephone: (0535) 645214

Below:
With the general withdrawal of BR's first-generation diesel railcars, the Railway acquired a two-car Class 108 set during the early 1990s. The set is seen at Haworth shed, in the company of diesel shunter No D2511 and main line diesels Nos D8031 and D5209.
K&WVR

The 957 Project.
*As BR No 52044, the engine leaves
Keighley with a Haworth train
on 22 March 1975, that year's
Enthusiasts' Day.*
Nigel Hunt

Below:
*An artist's impression of No 957 as it
will appear outshopped in L&YR
passenger livery, with the Club saloon
in tow.*
The K&WVR Trust

WORTH VALLEY

Trust the Worth Valley – Investing for the future . . .

The KWVR has exciting plans to transform the Line in the coming years . . .

A Carriage Shed to preserve our irreplaceable fleet of service coaches . . .

But only with your help can they begin to take shape.

We have the experience, the style and the Railway, and with **your** help we can secure its future well into the 21st century.

Please complete and return the forms overleaf - **and remember, unlike many share issues the Trust does not ask for a minimum contribution.**

. . . the installation of mechanical signalling at Keighley and Haworth.

The completion of loco 80002 and the construction of a Viewing Gallery at Haworth Loco Works.

Plans for these and many more essential projects are well advanced.

KEIGHLEY & WORTH VALLEY RAILWAY TRUST
The Railway Station, Haworth, Keighley BD22 8NJ
REBUILDING YESTERDAY, FOR TOMORROW, TODAY.

Below:
Currently undergoing repair for an early return to service is L&YR 0-6-0ST No 752, here seen shunting the engineer's yard at Oakworth in May 1981.
Dr John Sagar

Inset:
Nearing the end of a long-term overhaul and a return to steam is the ex-Taff Vale 0-6-2T, No 85. In this picture it is seen in the service of the former National Coal Board in the Durham coalfield where it was No 52. It is seen passing Philadelphia with a coal train from Herrington Colliery to Penshaw.
A. G. Castle

The K&WVR has waited before encouraging bookings for photo-charters. The gas lighting at Haworth makes for an especially attractive 're-creation' of a suburban train headed by No 80002 in November 1997.
John East

*I*n the following pictures we depart from some of the more familiar locations of Worth Valley trains, or else see where the photographers have attempted to extract something different from the scene...

5: Passing Images

Previous page above:
Leaving Keighley — well, that can't be changed, although this March 1983 picture uses stonework and girders to particular advantage. '4F' No 43924 sets out for Oxenhope. Lots of heads from windows? It's Enthusiasts' Day. The nearest coach is E43003, a BR non-gangwayed lavatory composite (I didn't make up the name).
W. A. Sharman

Previous page below:
The weather can be severe in the area but then the December of 1981 was exceptionally cold and snowy. A passer-by ignores both the photographer and the train which is bringing back to Keighley a trainload of rail excursionists from Sheffield. Diesel Vulcan *was a short-notice replacement for the '4F' which had failed.*
David Olsen-Hopper

Main Picture:
The sort of picture that the popular press of Edwardian years would have captioned Dignity and Impudence! No 34092 City of Wells *passes Ingrow in September 1982 as* Lord Mayor *potters in the yard.*
Brian Dobbs

Opposite:
The Ivatt tank has just passed Damems in this October 1973 picture, the composition of which is completed by the Midland lower-quadrant signal!
David Eatwell

Above left:
The camera lens produces tricks in this December 1983 shot of a Santa Special double-headed by the '4F' and the '8F'. Can you guess where it was taken?
Bob Avery

Below left:
Class 'A' headlamps for the Keighley-Oxenhope Express of the March 1990 Enthusiasts' Day, and a feeling that No 45596 Bahamas and its crew are really getting to grips with the 1 in 56 of Ingrow bank combine to provide a main line image.
Mike Taylor

Inset:
These really are passing images! The truly Victorian silhouette of L&YR
No 957, then running as BR No 52044, heading over Mytholmes Viaduct
with a passenger train, March 1975…
Dr John Sagar

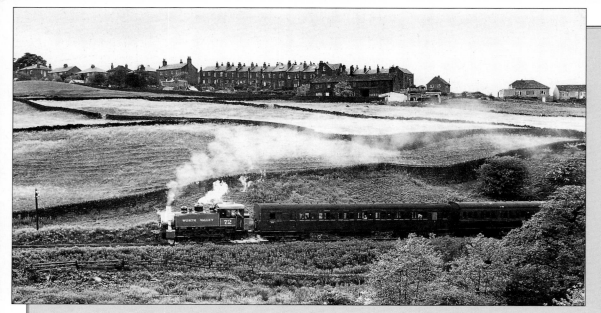

Above:
On 8 June 1968, when working a test train, the USA tank nears Haworth on the occasion of the official inspection of the line.
Anthony Cox

Left:
There are plenty of pictures of trains approaching the photographer at Mytholmes Tunnel — but fewer of a train about to be swallowed by encircling gloom! This is the inaugural special of 29 June 1968.
Les Nixon

Opposite:
This beautiful photograph was taken by a real steam professional, literally so for Jim Carter is a former BR fireman and driver. GN Atlantic Henry Oakley is fired-up ready for work at Haworth shed on 25 June 1977.
J. R. Carter

Haworth yard at the start of the 1980 Enthusiasts' Weekend.
J. R. Broughton

Opposite:
When you're travelling on a train the departure from Haworth provides nothing like the impression gained from the lineside. The Ivatt tank is bound for Oxenhope — and the date is 25 April 1971.
John Cooper-Smith

*I liked the photographer's caption so I haven't changed it at all.
'Standard Class 4 No 75078 briefly emerges from the freezing
fog between Haworth and Oxenhope, with a Santa Special on
12 December 1982. Double-heading with 75078 is
USA 2-8-0 Big Jim obscured by steam and fog.'*
Bob Avery

These days we have all become accustomed to preserved railways (or should we say heritage railways?) putting on complex timetables for special events. Some lines regularly offer summer peak timetables making use of three, or even four sets of coaches worked with four or more engines. These aim to cope with the demand from the general public who, after all, make up 80% of the people carried by the preserved lines.

6: A Look Behind the Scenes

But few lines fail to stage special events, usually held over both days of a weekend, when complicated services are provided often with unusual or hired-in locomotives, so as to attract railway enthusiasts. The railways' managers will say that such occasions are not particularly profitable but are run to boost the morale of the preservation society's members and railway operating staff, as well as contributing to the 'street cred' of the particular railway. The fact that the railway will derive 'free' publicity in the pages of the various railway journals as a result of photographs reproduced featuring the event is, of course, neither here nor there!

To provide an insight into the Keighley & Worth Valley Railway's current operations it seemed worth featuring the planning that went on for the organisation of one of the Railway's well-established Enthusiast Weekends.

The first of these took place on 17 March 1973, leading the Railway to claim that it invented the formula which Society pioneer, Mike Goodall, says was at first 'basically an excuse to steam as many of the forthcoming season's potential locomotives as possible to highlight any defects in them'.

At any rate, the annual enthusiasts' day first became a weekend and then a twice-yearly arrangement. The weekends became a major focus of the Railway's diary and through the mid/late 1970s sometimes attracted as many as 6,000 visitors, as well as featuring many weird and wonderful combinations such as a small industrial tank engine bucketing along the track as the pilot to American 2-8-0 *Big Jim*, with the latter's chime whistle echoing through the valley.

In time, the interest in the Enthusiasts' Weekends lessened. The Railway decided however to make a big feature of the 1998 event, as part of the celebrations to mark the 30th year of operation by volunteers. The autumn's big occasion would be the Worth Valley 30th Anniversary Weekend of 19/20 September.

How did the team go about the task of organising the Spring Enthusiasts' Weekend of 2/3 May 1998?

The first meeting principally dedicated to its organisation took place after lunch on 13 December of the previous year, and took place in the loft of the Vintage Carriages Trust's museum at Ingrow.

Those present were members of the Railway's Heritage Events Working Party of the Keighley & Worth Valley Railway. A month or so before, the Joint Management Committee of the K&WVR had considered the general outline of the proposed event. The special events recently staged by the Railway had met with such a favourable response that the Joint Management Committee was keen that something even bigger and better should be organised.

It had thrown out some ideas for consideration, hence this December meeting which was chaired by Co-ordinator, Heritage Events, David Pearson.

The meeting moved at a brisk pace. It was agreed that there would be three trains for public use — two of BR Mk 1 stock, one all-compartment, and the other all-corridor, the latter with the matching kitchen and restaurant cars to provide an on-train meals service. There had been favourable comment by enthusiasts at the previous operation of all-compartment and all-corridor trains.

With the visiting public showing increasing interest in the provision of the Vintage Train it was essential that this should be included, too. For much of the time on both days it would run only between Keighley and Ingrow, but it is agreed that there will be one round trip to Oxenhope and back, leaving Keighley at 15.10.

In fact, there will be two Vintage Train sets: one made up with two of the ex-Metropolitan coaches and, making a very rare appearance in service by special agreement of the owner, the ex-NER saloon, LNER No 21661. The vehicle is 127 years old and liable to damage. Public access must be by the public doors only. The other set will comprise LMS compartment third No 12066 and the ex-L&YR brake No 1474.

Finally, a goods train 'of appropriate vehicles' will be operated between Ingrow and

Above left:
The 'Pug' No 51218 descends towards Keighley and passes over the GN straight with the freight train on 3 May 1998.
Jim Winkley

Above:
Visiting Standard '4' No '75014' is pictured heading the corridor set at the Mound (between Damems loop and Oakworth) when working to Oxenhope on 3 May 1998. The front numberplate read No 75019, one cab side the same, the other 75014!
Jim Winkley

Keighley and back in the paths for the Vintage Train while this is away to Oxenhope and back. The demonstration goods train will be worked by recently restored Lancashire & Yorkshire Railway 'Pug', BR No 51218.

As to the other locomotives in use on both days, the operational fleet is expected to comprise the LNWR 'Coal Tank' No 1054 and the Great Western Railway pannier tank No 5775, both for use with the Vintage Train. If it is back in working order, the Vintage Carriages Trust's unique industrial 0-6-0 well-tank *Bellerophon* will be used. Built in 1874 at Haydock, Lancs it is the oldest engine on the Worth Valley.

To work with the two main train sets it is planned to use three engines, each of which is capable of hauling six coaches: home-based '4' 4-6-0 No 75078, '2' 2-6-0 No 78022, and '4' 2-6-4T No 80002. But this proposal has to be modified because someone points out that in fact 2-6-0 No 78022 is happy with a load of five coaches only and pushed beyond its limits with six.

The suggestion has been made that the Railway should publicise the event as featuring BR Standard locomotives. To add to their appeal the idea is that Standard Class '5' 4-6-0 No 73082 *Camelot* should be hired-in from the Bluebell Railway. The slogan for the event's promotion will on the lines of, 'We've got Standards to Maintain'. This is appropriate as 1998 is the 50th anniversary of the founding of British Railways. Also, the publicity will stress that not many preserved railways can turn out four BR Standard engines and two sets of restored Mk 1 coaches.

Are there any other engines that might be considered, asks someone at the meeting? Unfortunately, the *Bahamas* Locomotive Society's LMS 'Jubilee' No 45596 *Bahamas* will be 'out of ticket' as it is due to be withdrawn for major overhaul at the end of the year. A idea has been floated by a photographic charter group that East Lancs-based 'Crab' No 42765 should be hired-in to help recreate a Oxenhope-Morecambe excursion of times past. No one from the group turns up to the meeting so the proposal dies.

The sight of an engine being turned on Keighley turntable proved popular with the onlookers during the October events, so could this be repeated? It can, but locomotive diagrams will need to be arranged to suit. There are access problems for the heavier engines so only the smaller ones can be used. The new Keighley headshunt will be used but trains must not go beyond the site of the former buffer-stop as clearances have still to be checked.

John Downs of the Scammell Owners' Society is at the meeting to advise on how he and his colleagues can operate their characterful railway road vehicles to provide a collection and delivery parcels 'service' to stations. Proper uniforms will be worn and 'Fragile' packages will be trundled to and from the trains. There will have to be some restrictions on operations at stations, and only the non-corridor set with brake vans at each end will be met by the road vehicles.

There is enthusiasm for a vintage bus service, to be provided by vehicles from Keighley Bus Museum. The mainstay will be the unique Roe-bodied Bristol K5G, formerly of Keighley-West Yorkshire Services, which is owned and operated by Keighley & District Travel, and there will be another vehicle, to be provided by Keighley Bus Museum.

Vintage bus routes will need to be thought-out carefully because by then the road to Hebden Bridge will have closed for its year-long repairs, and there might be difficulties with the volume of diverted traffic.

Trains, railway goods vehicles and vintage buses — all at the meeting agree that the K&WVR will be able to offer a total transport experience and that this should be publicised accordingly.

But perhaps diesel enthusiasts will feel a little left out? With seven steam locos due to work on both days the first thought is that there will no chance for a diesel to be used as well. Then the suggestion is made — and adopted — that the diesel will be the last loco off Haworth shed and that it will work the Saturday evening trains. Either the Class 20 or the Class 25 will be chosen.

Present at the meeting is Nick Bennett, the K&WVR's Timetable Officer, who has to draw up the working timetable. The meeting registers unanimous approval at the idea that the timetable for the successful October special event should be repeated for the May weekend.

By mid-February Nick has produced draft working timetable No 2, setting out the timings, allocation of train sets to timetabled trains, locomotive hours and allocation, and ideas for double-heading. A Standard '5' will not be coming to the Railway, after all, so another BR Standard engine is being sought.

Two months after the draft timetable, and on 20 April David Pearson produces his Special Traffic Notice & Staff Information which runs to seven pages, the loco movements and staff shifts having been worked out by Keith Jones. The general basis of what was discussed and agreed in December has been maintained. Give or take one or two bodies, each day's operations call for eight engine crews, five guards, seven staff at Haworth Loco, 12 station staff, and three travelling ticket collectors.

There is helpful instruction for staff. Please ensure that before a locomotive goes on to a train at Keighley *it is facing chimney uphill:* 'A considerable number of complaints were received last time we turned locomotives and sent them uphill the "wrong way round" '.

By courtesy of its Heritage Rail Traction owners, the visiting Standard engine will be BR Standard '4' 4-6-0 No 75014, in its current disguise as No 75019. All told, at least eight engines will be provided to work the timetable on the Saturday and seven on the Sunday: four Standard engines, the 'Coal Tank', the 'Pug', either *Bellerophon* (if it is ready in time) or the GWR pannier tank, with the Class 20 diesel on the Saturday evening only. The diesel will work two return trips with the corridor set with one bar open, but no food service.

The spare loco in steam will be Stanier '8F' 2-8-0 No 48431. The turntable is indeed to be advertised as an attraction, and the engine moves to it have been worked out.

Some workings will be double-headed, with engines attached or detached at Haworth loop, and most permutations of Standard engines will be provided. The Vintage Train will make use of Platform 3 at Keighley and for most of the morning and early afternoon on both days there will be departures every 15min from both Keighley and Ingrow stations. This calls for everyone to be on their toes, with 100% train occupation on this lower stretch of the Railway.

John Downs and friends will be running their railway road vehicles serving the stations in the lower valley. The vintage bus service will be operated between Ingrow station and Oldfield, overlooking the 'real' Worth Valley. Haworth Band will be playing each day in

Ingrow Goods yard and the Vintage Carriages Trust will be offering 'on request' tours of its new workshops. Visitors will be informed that they can ask station staff at Oakworth and Damems stations to show them 'behind the scenes'.

The K&WVR Council has agreed that normal fares will apply, with Day Rovers increased to £8 or £16 for a family — no supplements and no charges for use of the bus service. The publicity goes for printing, with two leaflets — one outlining the features of the weekend, including short 'biogs' of the engines and also the bus timetables, the other setting out the working timetable.

And so to 2 May which is truly under way as we arrived at a grey, rather chilly Oxenhope. All is going to plan says David Pearson who is working Guard 2 duty. The only noticeable change is that *Bellerophon* is unavailable because the regulator of the '8F' had been blowing through and so this engine had to be the priority for attention. The 'Pug' was put through its paces with a train on 24 April when it passed its brake trial with flying colours.

The 14.10 from Keighley is indeed in the platform, on time, and headed by the two Standard Class '4' 4-6-0s which then make a fine sight as they run-round their train. The engines and set work another round trip together before, as planned, No 75078 is detached from the 16.10 ex-Keighley at Haworth loop.

At Oxenhope, the kitchen and restaurant cars are detached by No 75014 from the 17.35 arrival. It's not an easy manoeuvre. Hudswell Clarke diesel No 23 *Merlin* roars into life to shunt the detached vehicles in the yard. Away on time from Oxenhope behind the '4', at Damems loop the corridor set crosses the compartment set headed by Nos 78022 and 80002 which look very fine in tandem. At Ingrow, the pannier tank No 5775 and the 'Coal Tank' stand on the Vintage set, awaiting their path to run light to Haworth.

At Haworth, there is a pleasing line-up on shed of Nos 78022, 80002, 75078, 1054 and 48431. Class 20 No D8031 comes on to our train at Haworth loop and in turn No 75078 is detached from the return 19.00 ex-Oxenhope. The station gas-lamps come on, to add glowing distinction. K&WVR Chairman, Graham Mitchell joins us enthusiastically. 'It's gone really well. This diesel trip is a real bonus — it's really appreciated by the staff — you can see how everyone is enjoying it!'

Sunday's weather was better and the numbers were good, too — 1,600 passengers booked, 1,200 on Saturday but as the majority of ticket sales were Day Rovers the total passenger journeys for the weekend were computed as 6,000+.

An operating hitch during mid-morning Sunday meant that punctuality suffered until mid-afternoon. With blue-backed Polmadie shedplate and Caley-style route indicator, the 2-6-4T bustled impressively into Oakworth with the delayed 11.10 ex-Keighley and, as planned, at Oxenhope the visiting 4-6-0 came on as pilot.

We listened to Haworth Band at Ingrow, sampled the Roe-bodied Bristol K5G out to Oldfield and back and talked to John Downs about the hazards of driving 30-year-old Scammell mechanical horses in today's traffic. Mid-afternoon and the 'Coal Tank' looked a picture as it gyrated majestically on Keighley turntable. Next, Nos 78022 and 80002 raised the echoes as they propelled their stock out of the station for stabling so that the 'Coal Tank' and No 5775 could work the Vintage set to Oxenhope and back.

Below:
Tablet exchange at Damems.
Chris Dixon

At 16.10, the 'Pug' arrived on the freight train of three wagons and brake van to a delighted audience — the photographers were certainly out in force. The little saddletank looked even better as it stormed chimney-first up to Ingrow 45min later, by which time the passenger trains had recovered punctual running. The need to water both engines working the 17.10 ex-Keighley, however, had resulted in a delayed departure.

The day was beginning to wind down. The well-filled 17.10 from Oxenhope arrived behind No 75078, its companion 4-6-0 having been detached as booked at Haworth to go to shed, and the train set was now minus kitchen car which had been taken off for cleaning at Oxenhope. Then came an unscheduled working — the 'Coal Tank' and 5775 at the head of the LMS third, Lanky brake and 'Old Gentleman's Saloon', working Ingrow to Haworth in the bright evening sunshine. The little train made a memorable spectacle.

No 75078 worked the last train of the day, the 18.10 from Keighley which arrived on time at Oxenhope. It had been a good weekend!

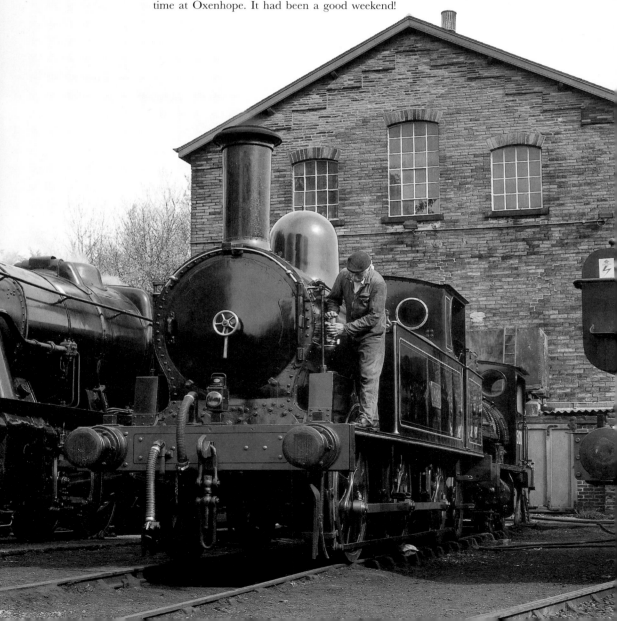

A chance to look at some of the engines that have visited the Worth Valley — in one or two cases, only just — and a reminder that it's a two-way traffic.

7: Visiting Celebrities

Previous page above:
Flying Scotsman *at Keighley for a filming assignment — the much satirised Hovis tv commercial, February 1980. The platform benches look dangerously placed.*
Terry Hanson

Previous page below:
Another big'un — Duchess of Hamilton *making polite conversation with 0-6-0T No 47279 which is working a demo goods. 20 October 1990.*
Dr John Sagar

Inset:
Hardly a traditional Great Western branch line, yet these two visitors look surprisingly at home: '4575' 2-6-2T No 5572 from Didcot Railway Centre waits at Oakworth with the 14.35 Keighley-Oxenhope, 12 April 1987...
Brian Dobbs

Right:
...into Oxenhope comes '61xx' 2-6-2T No 6106 (another Didcot-based engine) with a train from Keighley, 9 October 1988.
Brian Dobbs

BEWARE
OF
TRAINS.

Left:
Another engine that once worked to the South Coast — Butterley-based ex-Somerset & Dorset 2-8-0 No 13809, laying a smoke-trail on the approach to Oakworth, 8 April 1984.
Brian Dobbs

Below:
A line-up at Haworth at 07.30 on 16 March 1991, to record the visit of Southern Railway 'King Arthur' No 777 Sir Lamiel. US-built No 30072 was purchased by the SR and here carries a shed-plate that is a reminder of its days as Guildford shed pilot. The 'Coal Tank' completes the picture.
Robin Stewart-Smith

Such an improbable meeting that you can hardly believe it! Big Jim *stands alongside Liverpool & Manchester Railway 0-4-2* Lion *just outside Keighley station on 5 September 1981. No, they didn't double-head — the out of sight '8F' was* Big Jim's *train engine.*
David Olsen-Hopper

Below:
LNER-design 'K1' 2-6-0 No 2005,
normally based on the North Yorkshire Moors
Railway, makes a confident start from
Keighley on 27 March 1982.
Joma Enterprises

Right:
The Vintage Carriages Trust's Bellerophon
on tour — and about to leave Sheringham,
North Norfolk Railway, 6 September 1996.
Vintage Carriages Trust